Novell®

GroupWise 6.5

AF701183

Getting Started

GroupWise 6.5 Client Window

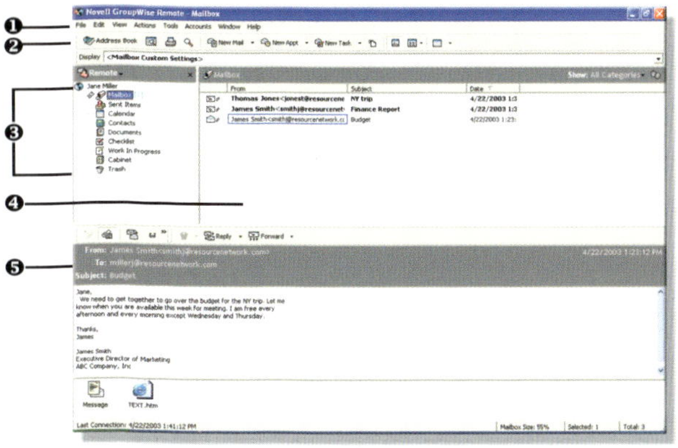

❶ **Menu Bar** – contains all the tools for use with Novell GroupWise 6.5 Client.
❷ **Main Toolbar** – contains shortcuts to common GroupWise tools.
❸ **Folder List** – displays your folders in a hierarchical view.
❹ **Item List** – displays the items in the selected folder.
❺ **QuickViewer** – displays the contents of the item selected in the Item List.

Folders List

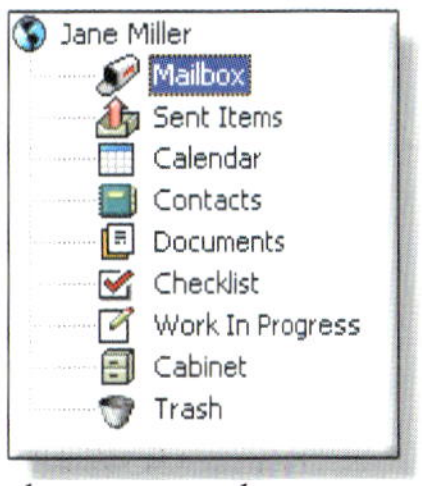

Mailbox – contains items that you have received.

NEW **Sent Items** – displays all sent items from the Mailbox and Calendar.

Calendar – contains a calendar for storing information about your appointments, notes, and tasks.

NEW **Contacts** – stores names, e-mail addresses, phone numbers, addresses, and other information about your contacts.

Documents – contains references to the documents that you have written, as well as the documents you have access to in the default library.

NEW **Checklist** – allows you to create a task list. You can also move other items such as messages or tasks to this folder.

Work In Progress – stores drafts of unsent messages and uncompleted items.

Cabinet – contains personal folders that you create.

Trash – contains deleted items.

NEW Using the Address Selector

When you are composing a new item, such as a Mail Message, you can address the item using the **Address Selector**.

1. Create the item and click the **Address** button.
2. Click the arrow on the **Look in address book** box.
3. Select an address book from the resulting menu.
4. Click the **To**, **CC**, or **BC** buttons, as appropriate.
5. Double-click each recipient that you want to include.
6. Click the **OK** button when you are finished.

Note: To remove a recipient, select the entry in the ***Selected*** *box and click the* ***Remove*** *button.*

Tabbed Item Views

NEW

Item views now have tabs where you can select options and specify additional information about the item. New items that you create, as well as items that you have received and sent provide tabs for additional options. Click on each tab to see the available options.

Sending and Retrieving Items

Using GroupWise, you can send and retrieve several different types of items, including: mail messages, appointments, tasks, reminder notes, and phone messages.

- To create a new item to send, select **New** from the **File** menu and select an item from the resulting menu. Fill out the information in the resulting dialog box and click the **Send** button.
- To send and retrieve items, select **Send/Retrieve** from the **Accounts** menu and select **All Marked Accounts** (or select the appropriate account) from the resulting menu.
- To read an item that you have received in your **Mailbox**, double-click the item.

Note: You can also view selected items in the ***QuickViewer****. To display the* ***QuickViewer****, click the* ***QuickViewer*** *button on the* ***Main Toolbar****.*

Using the Display List

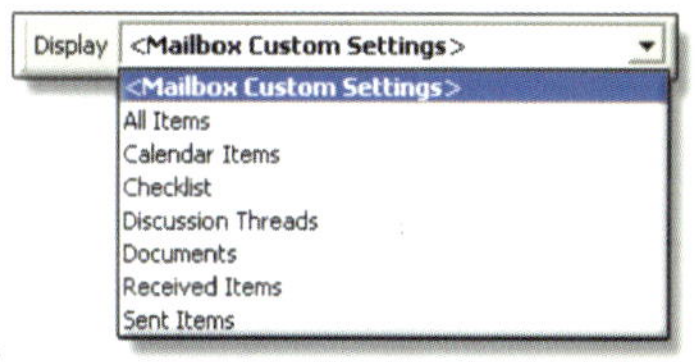

Use the **Display List** to change the way items are viewed in the **Item List**. To display the **Display List**, select **Toolbars** from the **View** menu, and select **Display Settings** from the resulting menu. Click the arrow on the **Display** box to select a display option.

Note: To make changes to the display options, select ***Display Settings*** *from the* ***View*** *menu, and select* ***Edit/Create*** *from the resulting menu.*

Categories

NEW

Assigning a Category to an Item

Categories help you organize your items. You can assign a category to any item, including contacts.

1. Right-click an item.
2. Select **Categories** from the pop-up menu.
3. Select a category from the resulting menu.

Note: To view items by category, click on the ***Show*** *menu in the upper-right corner of the* ***Item List****, and select the category name from the resulting menu.*

Creating a New Category

1. Right-click an item and select **Categories** from the pop-up menu.
2. Select **More** from the resulting menu.
3. Enter the category name in the text box at the bottom of the **Categories** box.
4. Click the **Add** button.
5. *Optional:* To assign a color to a category, select the category name and click on **Edit Color**. Click on a color and click **OK**.
6. Click the **OK** button when you are finished.

Working with Items

Creating a New Item

1. Select **New** from the **File** menu.
2. Select an item from the resulting menu.
3. Fill out the resulting form.
4. Click the **Send** or **Post** button.

Attaching a File

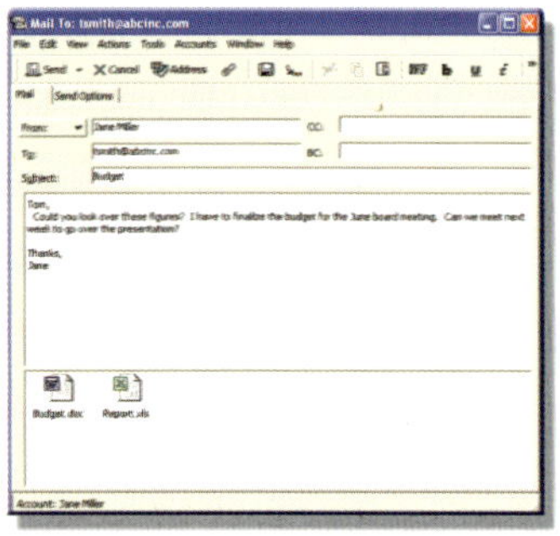

1. Create a new item.
2. Click the **Attach a File** button on the **Main Toolbar**.
3. Locate and select the **File** that you want to attach.
4. Click the **OK** button. An icon representing the item will appear in the lower pane.
5. Click the **Send** button when you are finished.

*Note: To delete an attachment, right-click the attachment icon and select **Delete** from the pop-up menu.*

Working with Attachments

1. When you receive an item with an attachment, open the item.
2. Right-click the attachment icon in the lower pane of the message window and select one of the following options:
   - *To view the attachment in the message pane,* select **View Attachment.**
   - *To view the attachment in a separate window,* select **View in New Window**.
   - *To open the attachment,* select **Open**. You may need to locate and select the application you want to use to open the item.
   - *To open with a particular application,* select **Open With**. Locate and select the application you want to use to open the attachment. Click the **OK** button.
   - *To save the attachment,* select **Save As**. Select the location where you want to save the attachment, and enter a name for the attachment in the **File name** box. Click the **Save** button.
   - *To print the attachment,* select **Print**. Select the item you want to print and select other print options. Click the **Print** button.

Changing the Item Type

You can convert any item in your **Mailbox** to another type of item. For example, you might want to change a mail message to an appointment.

1. In your **Mailbox**, select the item that you want to change.
2. Select **Change to** from the **Edit** menu.
   - *For posted items*, select an item type from the resulting menu.
   - *For group items*, select **More** from the resulting menu. In the **Change To** box that appears, select **Group** and then select the type of item you wish to change to.
3. Enter information, including recipient information.
4. Click the **Send** or **Post** button.

*Note: You can also right-click an item and select **Change to** from the pop-up menu. Make selections and click the **OK** button.*

NEW Adding a Subject to an Item

You can add a personalized subject to items in your **Item List**. This subject will be displayed in the **Item List** and the **Calendar**. The original subject will be displayed when you open the item.

1. Double-click the item in your **Mailbox** or **Calendar**.
2. Click on the **Personalize** tab.
3. Enter the new subject in the **My Subject** box.
4. Click the **Close** button.

Resending an Item

1. Click on the **Sent Items** folder in the **Folder List**.
2. Right-click the item that you want to resend.
3. Select **Resend** from the pop-up menu.
4. If the item that you want to resend is a recurring item, click the **This Instance** button or **All Instances** button.
5. *Optional:* Make changes to the item.
6. Click the **Send** button on the **Main Toolbar**.
7. Click **Yes** to retract the original item or click **No** to leave the original item in place.

Retracting an Item

Retracting a sent item will delete it from the recipient's **Mailbox**. You can retract an appointment, reminder note, or task at any time, but mail and phone messages can only be retracted if they have not been opened. Messages sent to a non-GroupWise mail system cannot be retracted.

1. Click on the **Sent Items** folder in the **Folder List**.
2. Select **Delete** from the **Edit** menu, press the **Delete** key, or right-click the item and select **Delete** from the resulting menu.
3. Select **Recipient's Mailbox**, or an appropriate mailbox, from the **Delete Item** dialog box.
4. Click the **OK** button.

Tracking Items

You can track your sent items to see when an item was delivered or opened. You can also view send options, such as priority, return notification, and reply requests.

1. In the **Sent Items** folder, select the item that you want to track.
2. Select **Properties** from the **File** menu, press **Alt + Enter**, or click the **Properties** button. The Properties window will appear, displaying the item's properties.

Printing an Item

1. Select the item that you want to print.
2. Select **Print** from the **File** menu.
3. Select the items and attachments that you want to print. To select multiple items, hold the **Ctrl** key while you click.
4. *Optional:* Check the **Print attachment with associate application** box to ensure proper formatting.
5. Click the **Print** button.

Deleting an Item

Deleted items are placed in the **Trash** until the **Trash** is emptied. To delete an item, select the item and press the **Delete** key.

*Note: If you delete an item from the **Sent Items** folder, the **Delete Item** dialog box will appear. Select the appropriate option and click the **OK** button.*

Retrieving a Deleted Item

1. Click on the **Trash** folder in the **Folder List**.
2. Select the item that you want to retrieve.
3. Select **Undelete** from the **Edit** menu. The item will be restored to the folder in which it was originally stored. If the original folder is not available, the item will be placed in the **Mailbox**.

*Note: You cannot retrieve items once the **Trash** has been emptied.*

Emptying the Trash

1. Right-click the **Trash** icon, as it appears in the **Folder List**.
2. Select **Empty Trash** from the pop-up menu.
3. Click the **Yes** button to confirm the deletion.

*Note: You can also open the **Trash** folder and click the **Empty Trash** button on the **Folder Context** toolbar.*

Reminder Notes

Scheduling a Personal Reminder Note

1. In the **Calendar** folder, click the arrow on the **Open Calendar** button and select a view from the resulting menu, or click the **Day** button on the **Calendar Toolbar**.
2. Double-click an empty space in the **Reminder notes** list.
3. Enter a subject in the **Subject** box.
4. Enter a start date, or click the **Calendar** button in the **Start date** box, and select a start date.
5. Enter note text in the text area.
6. Click the **Post** Post button.

Scheduling a Reminder Note for Others

1. Select **New** from the **File** menu.
2. Select **Reminder Note** from the resulting menu.
3. Enter recipient e-mail addresses or usernames in the **To** box, pressing the **Enter** key after each entry.
4. Enter a subject in the **Subject** box.
5. In the **Start date** box, enter the date that this reminder should appear in the recipients' calendars, or click the **Calendar** button in the **Start date** box, and select a date.
6. Enter the note text in the message text area.
7. Click the **Send** Send button.

Tasks

Creating a Personal Task

1. Click the arrow on the **Create New Task** New Task button and select **Posted Task** from the resulting menu. Or, in your **Calendar**, double-click an empty space in the **Tasks** list.
2. Enter a subject for the task in the **Subject** box.
3. *Optional:* Enter a priority. A task priority can consist of a character, number, or a character followed by a number (i.e. A, 1, C2, B3, etc.).
4. Click the **Calendar** button in the **Start date** box, and select a start date.
5. Click the **Calendar** button in the **Due on** box, and select a due date.
6. *Optional:* Enter a description of the task in the text area.
7. Click the **Post** Post button when you are finished.

Assigning a Task to Others

1. Click the **Create New Task** New Task button.
2. Enter recipient e-mail addresses or usernames in the **To** box, pressing the **Enter** key after each entry.
3. Enter a subject for the task in the **Subject** box.
4. *Optional:* Enter a priority.
5. Enter a start date, or click the **Calendar** button in the **Start date** box, and select a start date.
6. Enter a due date, or click the **Calendar** button in the **Due on** box, and select a due date.
7. Enter a description of the task in the text area.
8. Click the **Send** Send button when you are finished.

Marking a Task as Complete

1. In the **Calendar** folder, double-click a task as it appears in the **Tasks** list.
2. Check the **Completed** box, located in the bottom right corner.
3. Click the **Post** Post button.

*Note: In **Calendar** view, you can quickly mark a task as complete, by checking the box next to the task in the **Tasks** list.*

Appointments

Scheduling a Personal Appointment

You can post personal appointments so that other users will know when you are available.

1. Click the arrow on the **Schedule New Appointment** New Appt button on the **Main Toolbar** and select **Posted Appointment** from the resulting menu.
2. Enter appointment information in the spaces provided.
3. Click the **Post** Post button.

Sending an Appointment Request

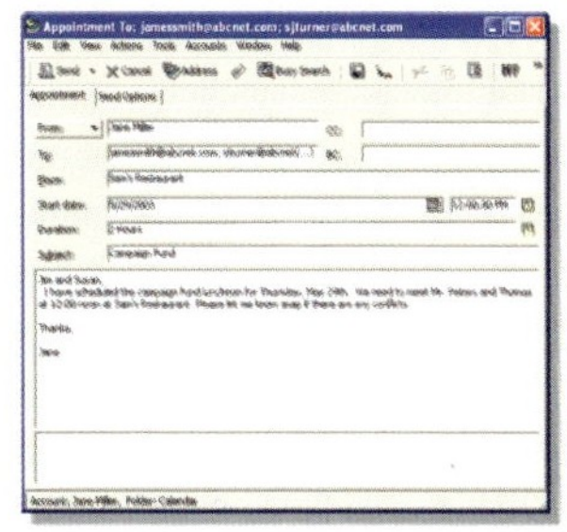

1. Select **New** from the **File** menu and select **Appointment** from the resulting menu, press **Ctrl + Shift + A**, or click the **Schedule New Appointment** New Appt button.
2. Enter recipient e-mail addresses or usernames in the **To** box, pressing the **Enter** key after each entry.
3. Enter a location description in the **Place** box.
4. Enter a start date, or click the **Calendar** button in the **Start date** box, and select a start date.
5. Enter a start time and duration in the spaces provided. Duration can be in minutes, hours, or days. You can also click the **Time** button, and drag the arrows on the sliding scale to select a duration. Use the green arrow to select a start time and use the red arrow to select an end time. Click the **OK** button.
6. Enter a subject in the **Subject** box.
7. Enter message text in the message text area.
8. Click the **Send** Send button when you are finished.

Rescheduling an Appointment

1. In the **Sent Items** folder, select the appointment you want to reschedule.
2. Select **Resend** from the **Actions** menu.
3. If the appointment is a recurring one, click the **This Instance** button or the **All Instances** button.
4. Make the necessary changes.
5. Click the **Send** Send button.
6. Click **Yes** to retract the original item.

Canceling an Appointment

1. In the **Sent Items** folder, select the appointment that you want to cancel.
2. Select **Delete** from the **Edit** menu.
3. If the appointment is a recurring item, click the **This Instance** button or **All Instances** button.
4. Check the **All Mailboxes** box.
5. Click the **OK** button.

Responding to an Appointment Request

1. Double-click the appointment request.
2. Click the **Accept** or **Decline** button.
3. *Optional:* Enter other information.
4. Click the **OK** button.

*Note: If the appointment is recurring, click the **This Instance** button to accept or decline this appointment occurrence. Click the **All Instances** button to accept or decline all instances of the recurring appointment.*

Documents

Creating a Library Document

When you create a new document in GroupWise, you are adding a document to a library. You can also add documents to a library by importing, copying, or checking in an existing document. You can base the new document on an application's template, a GroupWise template, or a file. The system administrator must set up the library and assign access rights.

1. Select **New** from the **File** menu and select **Document** from the resulting menu, press **Ctrl + D**, or click the **Create New Document** button.
2. Do one of the following:
   - Click **Select a GroupWise Template**, select a template in the list box, and click the **OK** button. *(To select a template from a different library, select the library from the drop-down list.)*
   - Click **Select a File**, and enter the name of the file you want to use, or click the **Browse** button to find the file. Click the **OK** button.
   - Click **Select an Application**, select the application that you want to use, and click the **OK** button.
3. Enter a subject in the space provided.
4. *Optional:* Click the **Properties** button to specify additional document information, such as the author or document type.
5. Click the **OK** button.

*Note: The documents that appear in your **Mailbox** are references to actual documents in a library.*

Checking Documents Out of a Library

You can check a document out of a library when you want to work on a document for an extended period of time. When you check a document out of a library, it is "locked." Other users can view a locked document, but cannot modify it.

1. In the **Mailbox**, select the document you want to check out.
2. Select **Check Out** from the **Actions** menu.
3. *Optional:* Enter a filename for the document in the **Checked Out Filename** box. *(If you don't specify a filename, GroupWise will use the document number as the filename.)*
4. In the **Checked Out Location** box, enter the path to the location where you want to store the checked-out document.
5. Click the **Check Out** button.

*Note: The changes you make to a checked-out document do not appear in the actual document until you check the document back in or update it. To check in a document, select **Check In** from the **Actions** menu.*

Address Book

The **Address Book** has been reorganized to display address books in an Address Book list. Groups are displayed below each expanded address book. The Address Book list consists of the **System Address Book**, the **LDAP Address Book**, the **Frequent Contacts Address Book**, and personal address books you create. To open the **GroupWise Address Book**, click the **Address Book** button on the **Main Toolbar**.

Using the Contacts Folder

NEW

By default, the **Contacts Folder** in the **Folder List** represents the **Frequent Contacts Address Book**. If you want the **Contacts Folder** to display entries from another address book, right-click the **Contacts Folder** and select **Properties** from the pop-up menu. Click the arrow on the **Address Book** box and select the address book. Click the **OK** button when you are finished.

Creating a Contact

1. Click on the **Contacts Folder** in the **Folder List**.
2. Select **New** from the **File** menu and select **Contact** from the resulting menu, or click the **New Contact** button.
3. Enter contact information such as name, e-mail address, and phone number.
4. *Optional:* Click the other tabs in the **New Contact** dialog box to enter additional contact information.
5. Click the **OK** button when you are finished.

Checklist

NEW

Working with the Checklist

- To create a master checklist, drag items to the **Checklist** folder.
- To create a new item in the **Checklist** folder, click the arrow on the **Create New Mail** button and select **Posted Message**. Enter a subject in the **Subject** box and enter text in the Message text area. Click the **Post** button.
- To arrange the items in the order that you want, click the **Checklist Toolbar** buttons , , , . If the **Checklist Toolbar** is not displayed, select **Toolbars** from the **View** menu and select **Folder Context** from the resulting menu.
- To assign a due date to an item in the **Checklist**, double-click the item to open it. Click on the **Checklist** tab. Click the **Calendar** button in the **Due on** box and select a due date. Click the **Close** button when you are finished.

Getting Help

Using the Help Contents

1. Select **Help Topics** from the **Help** menu, or press **F1**.
2. Click the **Contents** tab.
3. Double-click a **Book** icon to view section contents.
4. Click on a topic to view the help text.
5. *Optional:* Click on **Related Topics** in the display pane. Select a topic and click the **Display** button.

Using the Help Index

1. Select **Help Topics** from the **Help** menu, or press **F1**.
2. Click the **Index** tab.
3. In the first text box, enter the first few letters of the word you want to search for. **GroupWise Help** will try to find a match to your word as you type.
4. Select an index entry and click the **Display** button.

Using the Help Search

1. Select **Help Topics** from the **Help** menu, or press **F1**.
2. Click the **Search** tab.
3. In the first text box, enter a word or phrase that you want to search for.
4. Click the **List Topics** button.
5. Select an entry and click the **Display** button.

Using Context-Sensitive Help

1. Select a command from the menu bar. *(i.e select **Options** from the **Tools** menu.)*
2. Press the **F1** key on the keyboard. A help window will appear, displaying information about the feature that you are using.
3. Click your mouse once when you are finished to close the **Help** window.

Mail

Creating a New Mail Message

1. Click the **Create New Mail** New Mail button.
2. *Optional:* To change the From name, click the **From** button and select a name.
3. Enter recipient e-mail addresses or usernames in the **To** box, pressing the **Enter** key after each entry.
4. Enter a subject in the **Subject** box.
5. *Optional:* Enter recipient e-mail addresses or usernames in the **CC** or **BC** boxes to send carbon copies or blank carbon copies.
6. Enter message text in the message body.
7. Click the **Send** Send button to send the message.

Reading a Mail Message

1. Double-click the message that you want to read.
2. Click the **Close** Close button when you are finished.

Note: Click once on a message to view the message in the QuickViewer. If the QuickViewer is not displayed, click the ***QuickViewer*** *button on the* ***Main Toolbar****.*

Replying to an Item

1. Open the item you want to reply to.
2. Click the **Reply** Reply button.
3. Check the **Reply to sender** or **Reply to all (sender and recipients)** box.
4. *Optional:* Check the **Include message received from sender** box to include the text of the original message.
5. Click the **OK** button.
6. Enter reply text in the message body.
7. Click the **Send** Send button to send the reply.
8. Click the **Close** button to close the remaining open window.

Note: If you select ***Reply to all*** *and the original message contained BC recipients, your reply will not be sent to the BC recipients.*

Forwarding an Item

When you forward an item, it is sent as an attachment.

1. In your **Mailbox**, click the item that you want to forward.
2. Select **Forward** from the **Actions** menu.
3. Enter recipient e-mail addresses or usernames in the **To** box, pressing the **Enter** key after each entry.
4. *Optional:* Enter additional text in the message body.
5. Click the **Send** Send button.

Calendar

Viewing the Calendar

- *To view the* ***Calendar***, click on **Calendar** in the **Folder List**. Click the **Day**, **Week**, **Month**, **Year**, or **Multi-User** buttons on the **Calendar Toolbar** to select a view.
- *To view the* ***Calendar*** *in a separate window,* select **Calendar** from the **Window** menu and select a view from the resulting menu. Or, click the arrow on the **Open Calendar** button and select a view from the resulting menu.

Printing Your Calendar

1. Click the **Print Calendar** button on the **Main Toolbar**.
2. Select a calendar format, form, paper size, and orientation in the resulting dialog box. Click on the **Content** and **Options** tabs to select additional options.
3. *Optional:* Click the **Preview** button to see a preview of your printed **Calendar**. Click the **Close** button to close the preview.
4. Click the **Print** button.

Folders

Creating a Personal Folder

1. Select **New** from the **File** menu, and select **Folder** from the resulting menu.
2. Click on **Personal folder**, and click the **Next** button.
3. Enter a name for the folder in the **Name** box.
4. *Optional:* Enter a description in the **Description** box.
5. Click the **Up**, **Down**, **Right**, or **Left** buttons to position the folder in the **Folder List**, and click the **Next** button.
6. Specify display settings, such as which items to display and how they will be viewed.
7. Click the **Finish** button.

Creating a Shared Folder

1. Select **New** from the **File** menu, and select **Folder** from the resulting menu.
2. Click on **Shared folder**, and click the **Next** button.
3. Enter a name for the folder in the **Name** box.
4. *Optional:* Enter a description in the **Description** box.
5. Click the **Up**, **Down**, **Right**, or **Left** buttons to position the folder in the **Folder List**, and click the **Next** button.
6. Enter a username in the **Name** box and click the **Add User** button. Or click the **Address Selector** button, and click the arrow on the **Look in address book** box to select an address book. Double-click the username that you want to add and click the **OK** button.
7. Click on the user's name in the **Share List** and specify access options for the user.
8. Repeat steps 6 and 7 for each user you want to share the folder with and click the **Next** button.
9. Specify display settings, and click the **Finish** button.

Moving an Item

Click and drag the item from the **Item List** to the folder that you want. To keep a copy of the item in the original folder, hold the **Ctrl** key while you click and drag the item to the new folder.

Deleting a Folder

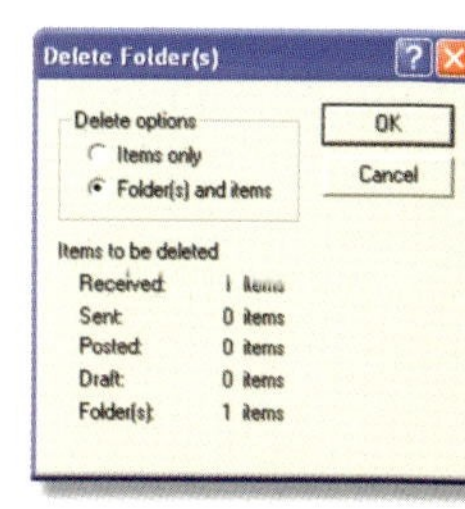

1. Right-click the folder that you want to delete.
2. Select **Delete** from the pop up menu.
3. Click on **Items Only** or **Folder(s) and items**.
4. Click the **OK** button.

QUICK Source

To order call toll-free 1-888-280-0424.

Visit our Web site: **www.resourcenetwork.com**

Customizing GroupWise

Using Junk Mail Handling

NEW

You can use **Junk Mail Handling** to filter unwanted Internet mail. You can block or junk e-mail from a specific user or from an Internet domain. This does not apply to internal e-mail where the sender is part of your GroupWise system.

1. To enable Junk Mail Handling, select **Junk Mail Handling** from the **Tools** menu.
2. On the **Settings** tab, check the appropriate boxes.
3. Click on the **Junk List**, **Block List**, and **Trust List** tabs to add e-mail addresses or domains to the appropriate list.
4. Click the **New** button to add a new e-mail address or domain to the list.
5. Enter an e-mail address or domain name in the text box and click the **OK** button.
6. Click the **Apply** button to apply changes.
7. Click the **OK** button when you are finished.

Note: Messages sent to a POP account are not eligible for this feature. Only Internet mail sent to your GroupWise account is eligible for Junk Mail Handling.

Customizing Toolbars

1. Right-click the toolbar that you want to customize. *(If the toolbar is not shown, select **Toolbars** from the **View** menu and select the toolbar from the resulting menu.)*
2. Select **Customize Toolbar** from the pop-up menu.
3. Select the way that you want to display toolbar buttons.
4. *Optional:* Select other display options.
5. Click the **Customize** tab.
6. In the **Categories** box, select the category of buttons you want.
7. Click once on the button that you want to add to the toolbar. A description of the button will appear at the bottom of the **Toolbar Properties** window.
8. Click the **Add Button** button, or click and drag the button to the location on the toolbar where you want to place the button.
9. Click the **OK** button when you are finished.

*Note: To remove a button from the toolbar, click and drag the button from the toolbar to the **Toolbar Properties** window.*

Switching Modes

Remote

To switch modes, click the arrow on the **Mode** drop-down list located on the **Folder List** header. Select a mode (**Online**, **Caching**, or **Remote**) from the resulting menu. You may be prompted to reboot for the new mode to take effect.

Discussions

Posting a Message to a Shared Folder

1. In the **Folder List**, click once on the shared folder you want to use.
2. Select **New** from the **File** menu.
3. Select **Discussion/Note** from the resulting menu. *(To post a different type of item, select **Change To** from the **Edit** menu and select the item type from the resulting menu.)*
4. Enter a subject in the **Subject** box.
5. Enter message text in the message text area.
6. Click the **Post** (Post) button when you are finished.

Replying to a Discussion

1. In a shared folder, select a discussion item.
2. Select **Reply** from the **Actions** menu.
3. Select a reply option. You can reply to the any item that you are reading or the original discussion topic. The reply will be posted in the shared folder, unless you choose to reply privately. If you choose to reply privately, the reply will only be sent to the individual who wrote the item and/or the recipients.
4. Click the **OK** button.
5. Enter your reply text in the message text area.
6. Click the **Post** (Post) button when you are finished.

Viewing Discussion Threads

In a shared folder, select **Display Settings** from the **View** menu, and select **Discussion Threads** from the resulting menu, or click the **View By** button and select **Discussion Threads**.

Shortcuts

Main Toolbar

Button	Shortcut	Menu
Address Book	none	Tools / Address Book
Properties	Alt + Enter	File / Properties
Print Calendar	none	File / Print Calendar
Find in GroupWise	Ctrl + F	Tools / Find
Create New Mail	Ctrl + M	File / New / Mail
Schedule New Appointment	Ctrl + Shift + A	File / New / Appointment
Create New Task	Ctrl + Shift + T	File / New / Task
Create New Document	Ctrl + D	File / New / Document
QuickViewer	Ctrl + Q	View / QuickViewer
View By	none	View / Display Settings
Open Calendar	none	Window / Calendar

New Item Toolbar

Button	Shortcut	Menu
Send	none	Actions / Send Using
Cancel	none	File / Close
Address	none	Actions / Address
Attach a File	Ctrl + L	File / Attachments / Attach File
Save	Ctrl + S	File / Save Draft
Change Item Type	none	Edit / Change to
Cut	Ctrl + X	Edit / Cut
Copy	Ctrl + C	Edit / Copy
Paste	Ctrl + V	Edit / Paste
Font	F9	Edit / Font / Font
Bold	Ctrl + B	Edit / Font / Bold
Underline	Ctrl + U	Edit / Font / Underline
Italic	Ctrl + I	Edit / Font / Italic
Spell Check	Ctrl + F1	Tools / Spell Check
Encrypt	none	Actions / Encrypt
Digitally Sign	none	Actions / Sign Digitally
HTML	none	View / HTML
Plain Text	none	View / Plain Text

ISBN 1-932104-07-0
9 781932 104073